Published in the United States
by Xist Publishing
www.xistpublishing.com
24200 Southwest Freeway
Suite 402- 290
Rosenberg, TX 77471

Hardcover ISBN: 978-1-5324-3207-1
Paperback ISBN: 978-1-5324-3206-4
eISBN: 978-1-5324-3205-7

Printed in the USA

xist Publishing

Would You Rather

Funny Questions, Conversation Starters and Situations

written by:

Stephanie Rodriguez

illustrated by:

Adam Pryce

Would you rather...

Be able to fly or breathe underwater?

Would you
rather...

Have a
pig snout
or a
pig tail?

Would you rather...

Have to dance or sing along any time you heard music?

Would you rather...

See a mermaid or a unicorn?

Would you rather...

Live in a sandcastle or a treehouse?

Would you rather...

Have Internet or air conditioning?

Would you rather...

Eat only spaghetti or only hot dogs for an entire year?

Would you rather...

Live without video games or live without TV?

Would you rather...

Go to mars or go to the moon?

Would you rather...

Be able to talk to dogs or talk to cats?

Would you rather...

Wear a snowsuit in the ocean or a swimsuit in the snow?

Would you rather...

Pet a porcupine or kiss a hedgehog?

Would you rather...

Always wake up before your alarm or always go to bed early?

Would you rather...

Have super hearing or super smelling?

Would you rather...

Sky dive or bungee jump?

Would you rather...

Only use a fork or only use a spoon?

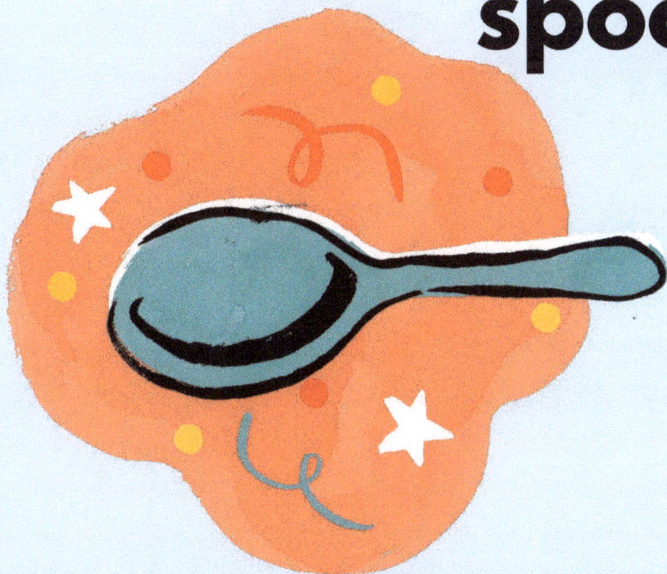

Would you rather...

Have sand in your bed or rocks in your shoes?

Would you rather...

Only wear one mitten or one shoe?

Would you rather...

Never eat tacos again or never eat pizza again?

Would you rather...

Go on a roller coaster or a water slide?

Would you rather...

Have a pet robot or pet alien?

Would you rather...

Read the book or watch the movie?

Would you rather...

Ride a tiger or a wolf?

Would you rather... Always have to wear shorts or always have to wear a sweatshirt?

Would you rather...

Be able to play the drums or play the guitar?

Would you rather...

Always wear a flower behind your ear

or a snake around your neck?

Would you rather...

Push a bike or carry a skateboard?

Send us your own
Would You Rather ideas:

wouldyourather@xistpublishing.com

www.ingramcontent.com/pod-product-compliance
Lightning Source LLC
LaVergne TN
LVHW070835080426
835508LV00031B/3466